BRYAN P. JESS

Understanding your finance

A Guide to Personal Financial Success

First edition

This book was professionally typeset on Reedsy
Find out more at reedsy.com

Contents

    1.

    2.

    3.

    4.

    5.

    6.

    7.

    8.

    9.

10.

11.

12.

13.

14.

Setting financial goals

A financial goal is a target an individual or organization sets to achieve a certain level of financial success. Setting financial goals is an important part of financial planning and can help individuals organize their finances and plan for the future.

When setting financial goals, it is important to think about the long-term and short-term goals. Long-term goals are usually 10-20 years away and may include paying off a mortgage, saving for retirement, or buying a house. Short-term goals are usually 3-5 years away and may include paying off credit card debt, saving for a vacation, or starting an emergency fund.

An individual should also consider their financial risk tolerance when setting financial goals. This is the amount of risk an individual is willing to take to achieve their goals. For example, an individual may choose to invest in stocks to achieve their goals, which can be risky but also potentially more profitable.

Financial goals provide a road map and help to keep you on track towards achieving your financial dreams. Financial goals can be short-term or long-term, and should be tailored to your individual situation.

Next, decide on the type of goals you want to set. Are you looking to save for retirement, buy a house, or save for a major purchase? Each goal should have a set time frame and dollar amount attached to it.

After setting your goals, it is important to create a plan to achieve them. This should include a budget, savings plan, and investment strategy. Make sure to review and adjust your plan as needed to ensure you are meeting your goals.

Setting financial goals can help you stay focused and motivated on your financial journey. With .a plan in place, you can take steps towards achieving your financial dreams.

Finally, an individual should also consider their budget when setting financial goals. This is the amount of money an individual has available to spend and save each month. Budgeting is important for achieving financial goals, as it can help an individual stay on track and prioritize their spending and saving.

Overall, setting financial goals is an important part of financial planning and can help individuals organize their finances and plan for the future. By considering their financial risk tolerance and budget, individuals can set achievable goals and work towards achieving them.

Steps to setting your financial goals.

1. Your Goals: Before you can set financial goals, you need to identify what you want to achieve. Consider your short-term and long-term goals. Think about things like retirement, buying a house, starting a business, or saving for a vacation.

2. Set a Budget: Once you have identified your goals, it's time to create a budget. Sit down and make a list of your expenses and income. This will help you determine how much money you have to work with and how much is available to put towards your goals.

3. Make a Plan: Once you have identified your goals and have a budget in place, create a plan to achieve them. This could include investing in stocks, creating a savings plan, or reducing your spending.

4. Track Your Progress: Make sure to keep track of all your expenses and income. This will help you stay on track and motivate you to continue working towards your goals.

5. Celebrate Success: Last but not least, make sure to celebrate your successes! Celebrating your successes will help you stay motivated and on track with your financial goals. Whether it's a small achievement or a major milestone, be sure to celebrate it.

One

Understanding Your Finances

Understanding your finances

1. How to Develop a Financial Plan: A Step-by-Step Guide

2. The Basics of Budgeting: How to Track and Manage Your Money

3. Investing 101: A Beginner's Guide to Investing in the Stock Market

4. How to Reduce Your Debt and Improve Your Credit Score

5. Retirement Planning: How to Start Saving for Retirement

6. Tax Planning: Strategies to Maximize Your Refund

7. Understanding Insurance: What You Need to Know

8. Advantages of Having an Emergency Fund

9. How to Create a Financial Safety Net

10. Managing Your Finances for Long-Term Financial Security

How to Develop a Financial Plan: A Step by Step Guide

Step 1: Assess Your Current Financial Situation

The first step in developing a financial plan is to assess your current financial situation.Taking a look at your current financial situation will help you identify areas that need improvement and areas where you may need additional support.

Step 2: Set Financial Goals

Once you have assessed your current financial situation, it's important to set financial goals. both short-term and long-term goals. Examples of short term goals are very important include saving for a down payment on a house, paying off debt, or starting a new business. Long-term goals could include saving for retirement, establishing an emergency fund, or investing in the stock market.

Step 3: Make a Budget

Budgeting is one of the major parts of any financial plan. It helps you track your income and expenses and ensure that you are staying within your financial means. To create a budget, you will need to list all your income and expenses, and then determine how much money you can allocate to each category. You should also consider setting aside money for savings and emergency funds.

Step 4: it's important to understand the basics of investing, including the difference between stocks and bonds, the different types of investments, and the risks associated with each.

Step 5: Manage Your Debt

Debt can be a major obstacle to financial success. To manage your debt, it's important to understand the types of debt you have and create a plan to pay it off. This could include transferring balances to a credit card with a lower interest rate or consolidating debt into a lower-interest loan.

Step 6: Protect Yourself with Insurance

Having the right insurance policies in place is an important part of any financial plan. There are a variety of insurance types, including life, health, auto, and homeowners insurance. It's important to understand the types of coverage you need and shop around for the best rates.

Step 7: Monitor Your Progress

Once you have a financial plan in place, it's important to review it regularly. This will help you track your progress and make sure that you are staying on track with your financial goals. It's also important to review your financial plan to ensure that it still meets your needs.

Developing a financial plan is a great way to ensure that you are on track to achieve your financial goals. By following these steps, you can create a personalized financial plan that will help you reach your goals and improve your financial security.

The Basics of Budgeting: How to Track and Manage Your Money

Budgeting is an essential part of financial management. It can help you understand what money you have coming in and what money you have going out. It also allows you to see where you can make changes to save money and build your savings. If you're new to budgeting, here are the basics of how to track and manage your money.

First, you need to understand your income sources. List all of your regular income sources, such as wages from a job, government benefits, investments, etc. Then, list all of your irregular income sources, such as bonuses, gifts, or refunds. When you have your income sources listed, you can add up the total. This will give you a better understanding of how much money you have to work with each month.

Next, you need to keep track of your expenses. Make a list of all of your regular expenses, such as rent, utilities, and groceries. Then, list all of your irregular expenses, such as travel, entertainment, and gifts. When you have your expenses listed, add up the total. This will give you a better understanding of how much money you have going out each month.

Now that you have a better understanding of your income and expenses, you can start creating a budget. A budget is a plan for how you will manage your money each month. Start by setting up a budget template, which will help you keep track of your spending. When setting up a budget template, be sure to include categories for fixed expenses (such as rent or mortgage payments), variable expenses (such as groceries or entertainment), and savings. Set up your budget template so that you are spending less than you are earning each month.

Once you have your budget template set up, it's time to start tracking your spending. Record every purchase you make and compare it to your budget template. This will help you identify any areas where you can save money. Additionally, you can use budgeting tools, such as apps or spreadsheets, to help you track and manage your money more efficiently.

Budgeting is an essential part of financial management. By understanding your income and expenses, setting up a budget template, and tracking your spending, you can make sure you're on the right path to financial success.

3.Investing in the Stock Market

Investing in the stock market can be a great way to grow your wealth and secure your financial future. It is important to do research before investing and to develop a strategy that fits your goals and risk tolerance.

When investing in stocks, it is important to understand that there are both short-term and long-term opportunities. Short-term investments may be based on short-term market trends, while long-term investments are typically based on a company's fundamentals and the expectation that the company will continue to grow and be profitable in the future.

It is also important to diversify your portfolio when investing in stocks. Diversification means investing in a variety of different stocks and other asset classes. This way, if one stock or sector falters, you will have other investments to balance out the loss and help protect your overall portfolio.

Before investing in stocks, it is also important to understand the associated risks. There is always a risk that you may not make money, or even lose money, on your investment. Therefore, it is important to educate yourself about the stock market and invest responsibly.

Finally, it is important to remember that investing in the stock market is a long-term commitment and requires patience. Over time, the stock market will go up and down, but as long as you remain disciplined and follow your strategy, you should be able to make money in the long run.

4. Benefits of having an emergency fund.

Having an emergency fund can provide a lot of financial security and peace of mind in the face of an unexpected event. Here are some of the main benefits of having an emergency fund:

1. Financial Security: An emergency fund gives you a cushion to fall back on in the event of an unforeseen emergency like a job loss, medical emergency, or home repair. It's a great way to buffer

yourself from the risks of life without having to rely on credit cards or take out a loan, which can add to your financial burden.

2. Peace of Mind: Having an emergency fund in place can help alleviate some of the stress and worry that comes with unexpected events. Knowing that you have a fund to draw from in the event of an emergency can help you feel more secure and in control of your finances.

3. Financial Goals: Having an emergency fund can also help you reach longer-term financial goals. You can use the money in your emergency fund to save for a house, car, or other big purchase. By setting aside money in your emergency fund, you can reduce the amount of money you need to borrow for large expenses.

4. Flexibility: An emergency fund gives you more flexibility in your finances. If you have cash on hand, you can choose how to use it instead of having to wait on a loan or other financing option. This can help you take advantage of opportunities that require quick action.

Overall, having an emergency fund is a great way to protect your finances and provide you with the peace of mind that comes with knowing you have a financial buffer when unexpected events occur.

5.How to Create a Financial Safety Net

Creating a financial safety net is an important part of any financial plan. It is an essential part of protecting your family and your assets in case of an unexpected event. Here are some steps to help you create a financial safety net:

1. Make sure you have adequate insurance coverage. Make sure you have life, health, and disability insurance, as well as property and liability insurance to protect your assets and your family in case of an unexpected event.

2. Build an emergency fund. This will help you keep your finances afloat in case of a job loss or other unexpected event.

3. Invest in stocks and bonds. Investing in stocks and bonds can help you build long-term wealth. It's important to make sure you have a diversified portfolio to lessen the risk of any one stock or bond losing value.

4. Consider setting up a Roth IRA. A Roth IRA can help you save for retirement and also provide a source of income in case of an emergency.

5. Create a budget and stick to it. Creating a budget and sticking to it can help you save money and build wealth over time. It can also provide stability in case of an unexpected event.

Creating a financial safety net is an important part of any financial plan. By following the steps above, you can create a safety net that will help you protect your family and your assets in case of an unexpected   event.

Two

Creating a budget

A budget is a tool that allows you to track your income and expenses, plan for the future, and make decisions about how to manage your money.

When creating a budget, the first step is to calculate your income. This includes salary, investments, and any other sources of income. track your expenditure,This includes bills, loan payments, and other necessary expenses. It is also important to set financial goals and set a spending limit. Lastly, it is important to monitor and adjust your budget as needed.

There are several benefits to budgeting. Budgeting can help you achieve financial security, increase your savings, and reduce financial stress.

Benefits of Budgeting

A. Improved financial security :Improved financial security is the result of taking steps to reduce financial risk, increase financial stability, and build long-term wealth. These steps can include budgeting, saving, investing, and reducing debt. By taking these steps, individuals can establish a solid foundation for achieving their financial goals.

Budgeting is an essential component of financial security. A budget allows individuals to track their spending, identify areas where they can cut back, and prioritize financial goals. A budget also provides a road map for staying within a predetermined spending limit and avoiding overspending.

Saving is also important for achieving financial security. Individuals should set aside money each month to build an emergency fund. This fund can be used to cover unexpected expenses and keep individuals from taking on debt. Additionally, saving for retirement is critical for building long-term wealth.

Investing is another way for individuals to improve their financial security. Investing can be done through stocks, bonds, mutual funds, and other vehicles. By investing in a diversified portfolio, individuals can reduce their risk and increase potential returns.

Reducing debt is another important step for improving financial security. Reducing debt can be done by making payments on time, paying more than the minimum balance, and negotiating with creditors for lower interest rates or longer repayment terms.

By taking these steps, individuals can improve their financial security and build long-term wealth. With proper planning, individuals can achieve their financial goals and enjoy greater peace of mind.

B. Increased savings :Increased savings can be a great way to build financial security. Saving money can help you reach your financial goals faster and give you peace of mind that you have a cushion to fall back on in case of an emergency. Increased savings can also be beneficial for retirement planning, allowing you to put more money away for future expenses.

One way to increase savings is to create a budget and stick to it. When you have a budget and understand your income and expenses, you can better plan for how much you can save. You can also look for ways to cut expenses, such as reducing the amount you spend on dining out, shopping, or entertainment.

Another way to increase savings is to increase your income. Consider taking on additional part-time or freelance work to boost your income. You can also look into ways to save money on taxes, such as taking advantage of tax deductions and credits.

Finally, automated savings can be a great way to increase your savings. Setting up automatic transfers from your checking to your savings account can help you save without even thinking about it. You can also set up rules like the 50/30/20 budgeting rule, which suggests that you save 20% of your income and allocate the remaining 50% for necessities and 30% for discretionary spending.

Increasing your savings can be difficult, but with the right strategies and dedication, you can achieve your savings goals and build the financial security you need.

C. Reduced financial stress :Reduced financial stress is a state of being where one is able to better manage their finances and overall financial health. This state can be achieved through a variety of methods, one being budgeting. Having a budget can help to ensure that one's income is being used responsibly and that all expenses are accounted for. Additionally, creating an emergency fund is another important step towards reducing financial stress. Having an emergency fund can help to provide security in the event of an unexpected expense or financial emergency.

Other methods of reducing financial stress can include setting and maintaining financial goals. Having a specific goal in mind, such as saving for retirement, can provide a sense of direction and motivation. Additionally, it can also be helpful to track progress towards financial goals and to develop strategies to help stay on track.

Finally, reducing financial stress can also involve seeking professional help and advice. Financial advisors, counselors, and even online courses can be a valuable source of knowledge and can help to provide a clearer understanding of one's financial situation. These resources can help to provide guidance and strategies for managing finances and reaching financial goals.

Reducing financial stress is an important step towards achieving financial security and independence. With the right strategies and resources, anyone can take the necessary steps towards achieving a more secure financial future.

Conclusion

A. Reiterate why budgeting is important :Reiterate why budgeting is important

Budgeting is an important tool for anyone to use in order to manage their finances properly. It is a way to track spending, set financial goals, and plan for the future. By budgeting, individuals can ensure that they have enough money to cover all of their expenses, while still having money left over to save or invest. Budgeting also helps individuals better understand their spending habits and make better decisions about where their money is going.

Budgeting is important because it helps individuals to live within their means. By setting a budget, individuals can limit their spending, which helps them to avoid debt and overspending. A budget also allows individuals to track their spending, as well as plan for future expenses such as holidays, car repairs, or medical bills. Budgeting can also help individuals to prioritize their spending and ensure that they are spending money on the things that are most important to them.

In addition, budgeting is important because it can help individuals to save money. By tracking their spending, individuals can identify areas where they can cut back and save more money. Budgeting also allows individuals to make sure they are saving enough money to reach their financial goals, such as retirement or a down payment on a house.

Overall, budgeting is an important tool for anyone to use in order to manage their finances properly. It can help individuals to limit their spending, track their spending, and plan for the future. In addition, budgeting can help individuals to save money and reach their financial goals.

B. Encourage readers to begin budgeting:Budgeting is an important part of financial health and success. It's a way to track where your money is going and to ensure that you stay on top of your expenses and meet your financial goals. Unfortunately, many people are intimidated by the idea of budgeting or simply don't know where to start.

If you're looking to encourage your readers to take control of their finances and begin budgeting, here are a few tips:

1. Start small. Don't try to overhaul your entire budget in one fell swoop. Start by focusing on small, achievable goals and gradually build from there.

2. Set realistic goals. Don't set yourself up for failure by setting unrealistic expectations for yourself. Set goals that are achievable and that you can stick to.

3. Live within your means. Avoid overspending on unnecessary items and focus on only buying what you need.

4. Be flexible. Life happens and budgets can change. Be willing to adjust and adapt to changing circumstances.

5. Get help. Don't be afraid to reach out for help if you need it. There are plenty of resources available to help you understand budgeting and stay on track.

With a little effort and planning, budgeting can help you to better manage your finances and save money in the long run. Take the time to create a budget and stick to it.

Three

Controlling debt

Controlling debt is the process of managing and reducing debt to improve overall financial health. It involves budgeting, understanding interest rates and fees, and developing a plan to pay off debt. The goal of controlling debt is to reduce the amount of debt owed and to eventually become debt-free.

Debt can be a major source of financial stress and can have a significant impact on your financial well-being. Fortunately, there are a variety of strategies available for controlling debt and regaining financial stability. In this article, we will discuss the key steps for controlling debt and take a look at how to use these strategies to achieve a healthier financial future.

1.Identify the Types of Debt You Have - The first step in controlling debt is to identify the types of debt that you have. This includes credit card debt, loans, mortgages, and any other debts that you may have taken on. Once you have identified the types of debt, you can begin to develop a plan for controlling it.

2.Consider Debt Consolidation - One option for controlling debt is to consolidate your debt into one monthly payment. This can help simplify the process of paying off your debt and may help you save money in the long run.

3.Make Payments to Creditors - Making regular payments to creditors is essential for controlling debt. Make sure to pay more than the minimum payment, as this will help you pay off your debt faster.

4.Look Into Refinancing Options - Refinancing your debt can help you save money by lowering the interest rates on your loans or mortgages. This can help reduce the amount of money that you are paying in interest each month and make it easier to pay off your debt.

5.Understand Interest Rates and Fees: Learn about the various types of interest rates and fees associated with debt and how they can affect the total cost of borrowing.

6.Develop a Plan to Pay Off Debt: Create a plan to pay off debt in a manageable and timely manner. Consider all options such as debt consolidation, refinancing, and negotiating with creditors.

7.Monitor Credit Reports: Monitor credit reports and scores regularly to ensure they are accurate and up-to-date.

8.Avoid Taking on Additional Debt: Avoid taking on additional debt unless absolutely necessary and only if it can be paid off quickly.

9.Seek Professional Advice: If needed, seek professional advice from a financial advisor or debt counselor to help develop a plan to pay off debt.

10.Earn extra income by starting a side hustle or creating passive income streams,Save Start an emergency fund to help pay off debt if needed.

Four

Building good credit

F actors for Building Good Credit

5 different types of credit

Establishing a Good Credit Score

Establishing Credit History

Paying Credit Card Bills On Time

Keeping Credit Card Utilization Low

Avoiding Excessive Applications for Credit

Managing Credit Responsibly

Reducing Credit Card Balances

Reviewing Your Credit Reports

Disputing Errors on Credit Reports

Resolving Credit Disputes

Monitoring Your Credit Score

Protecting Your Credit

Safeguarding Your Personal Information

Reporting Fraudulent Activity

Freezing our Credit

Avoiding Bad Credit Habits

Building good credit: is a crucial step in improving your financial situation and achieving financial stability. Good credit helps to open up access to financial products such as loans, mortgages and credit cards, as well as potentially improving your ability to negotiate more favorable terms on existing accounts. Building good credit takes time and patience, but it can be done.

becoming familiar with the different types of credit scores. Knowing what is being used to determine your credit score is essential to understanding how to improve it. Knowing the types of activities that can affect your credit score, such as regularly paying bills on time and avoiding excessive debt, is also important.

Credit is a form of financial agreement between an individual or business (the borrower) and a lender, such as a bank, that allows the borrower to access funds in exchange for payments over a set period of time. Credit is often used to purchase items or pay for services. Understanding how credit works is essential to making informed decisions about how and when to use it.

When borrowing money, it is important to understand the terms of the loan. This includes understanding the type of credit used, the interest rate, the repayment schedule, and any penalties for late payments. It is important to understand if the loan is secured or unsecured, as this can affect the interest rate and repayment terms. It is also important to understand the impact of the loan on an individual's credit report and score, as this can affect future borrowing opportunities.

Many lenders will require a credit check before approving a loan. A credit check is a review of an individual's credit history and credit score, which is used to assess the creditworthiness of the borrower. It is important to understand how credit scores are calculated and what factors can affect them, such as payment history, amount of debt, and length of credit history.

Finally, it is important to understand Understanding credit is essential for making responsible financial decisions. It is important to be aware of the potential risks and rewards of using credit and to be mindful of the repayment terms and potential consequences of failing to meet them. Borrowers should also be aware of the impact of using credit on their credit score and rating, as this can affect future borrowing opportunities.

Next, consider opening a secured credit card. This type of credit card requires a security deposit upfront, but it can help you begin to build a positive payment history. Make sure to use the card responsibly and pay the balance off in full each month.

If you're unable to get a secured card, you may want to consider becoming an authorized user on an existing account. This means you can use the account, but your activity will not be reported to the credit bureaus.

Finally, avoid taking out credit you don't need and make sure to pay your bills on time. This is the most important factor in building good credit, as it shows lenders that you are responsible with your finances.

Building good credit is a long-term process and it requires patience and dedication. However, by taking the right steps and making sure to stay on top of your credit, you can eventually improve your credit score and open up access to financial products.

Factors for Building Good Credit:

1. Make your payments on time: Being consistent with paying your bills on time is the most important factor in building good credit. Payment history accounts for 35% of your credit score and late payments can have a major negative impact.

2. Keep credit utilization low: This means to not use too much of your available credit. It's recommended to keep your credit utilization ratio below 30% and ideally closer to 10%.

3. Don't open too many accounts at once: Having too many new accounts in a short period of time can be a red flag to creditors that you're trying to take on too much debt.

4. Use a variety of credit products: Try to use a variety of different types of credit, such as credit cards, store cards, personal loans, and secured loans. This will show creditors that you can manage different types of credit responsibly.

5. Monitor your credit: It's important to regularly check your credit reports and make sure there are no errors or discrepancies. If there are, dispute them immediately.

6. Don't close unused credit cards: Closing accounts can have a negative effect on your credit score, even if the accounts are inactive. It's better to keep the accounts open and simply not use them.

Credit is a type of loan that can be used to make purchases, cover expenses, and even establish a credit history.

5 different types of credit

There are various types of credit available, depending on the purpose for which it is needed.

These are the five different types of credit available. Depending on the purpose for which it is needed, the right type of credit can be used to make purchases, cover expenses, and establish a credit history.

1. Revolving Credit: Revolving credit is a type of credit that allows the borrower to use up to a certain amount of credit and then repay

the amount over an extended period of time. The borrower can pay off the total amount or make partial payments.

2. Installment Credit: Installment credit is a type of credit that requires the borrower to make regular payments over a set period of time. This type of credit is typically used to purchase large items, such as furniture, appliances, or cars.

3. Secured Credit: Secured credit is a type of credit in which the borrower pledges an asset, such as a home or vehicle, as collateral for the loan. This type of credit typically has a lower interest rate than unsecured credit because the lender has a form of security should the borrower default on the loan. Examples of secured credit include mortgages, auto loans, and home equity loans.

4. Unsecured Credit: Unsecured credit is a type of credit in which the borrower does not have to pledge any collateral to secure the loan. This type of credit typically has a higher interest rate than secured credit because the lender does not have any form of security should the borrower default on the loan. Examples of unsecured credit include personal loans, credit cards, and lines of credit.

5. Peer-to-Peer Credit: Peer-to-peer credit is a type of credit that is provided by individuals, rather than traditional financial institutions. This type of credit is typically used for small loans or to cover short-term expenses. Examples of peer-to-peer credit include online lending platforms, such as Prosper and Lending Club.

Establishing a Good Credit Score:Establishing a good credit score is important for many reasons. It can help you secure a loan, get a lower interest rate, and even improve your chances of being approved for a job. Here are some tips for establishing and maintaining a good credit score:

1. Pay your bills on time.Make sure to pay all of your bills on time each month.

2. Keep your credit utilization ratio low. Your credit utilization ratio is the amount of credit you are using relative to your total credit limit. Try to keep it below 30%.

3. Monitor your credit report. I'm

4. Limit your application for new credit. Every time you apply for a loan or credit card, it can have a negative impact on your credit score.

5. Avoid maxing out your credit cards. If you do use your credit cards, make sure to pay them off in full each month.

6. Be careful with co-signing. Co-signing for someone else loan can have a negative impact on your credit score if they fail to make payments.

7. Don't close old accounts. Closing an old account can negatively affect your credit score.

By following these tips, you can establish and maintain a good credit score. This will help you qualify for better loan terms and even increase your chances of getting the job you want.

Establishing Credit History:Establishing a good credit history is an important part of financial stability. It is important to monitor your credit score regularly and make sure that you are making payments on time. A good credit score can help you get approved for a loan or a credit card with better terms and lower interest rates. It can also help you secure a job or a rental property.

Establishing credit history can take some time, but it's important to be patient and proactive.Examine your credit report from each of the three major credit bureaus the for any inaccuracies or outdated information. Dispute any errors with the credit bureau and make sure to follow up to ensure the corrections are made.

Once any errors on your report have been corrected, you can begin to build your credit history.open a secured credit card account. This is a great option if you don't have any credit history yet, as it allows you to make purchases while building your credit score. Make sure to pay the balance off in full each month so you don't incur any interest charges.

Another great way to establish credit is by taking out a loan. Consider taking out a small loan from a credit union or community bank.

Paying Credit Card Bills On Time:Paying credit card bills on time is one of the most important steps to maintaining a healthy credit score. Making timely payments shows lenders that you are a responsible borrower and can manage your debt appropriately. Additionally, when you pay your credit card bills on time, you avoid costly late fees and interest charges.Most credit card companies report late payments to the three major credit bureaus. This can result in a drop in your credit score, which will make it more difficult to get approved for loans or credit cards in the future.

It is important to make sure you can pay your credit card bills on time each month. Make sure you are aware of the due date for each bill and plan ahead. You may also want to set up automatic payments to ensure your bills are paid on time each month.

If you find yourself unable to pay your credit card bills on time, contact your credit card company immediately. Many companies have programs that allow you to make a reduced payment or extend the due date. This can help you avoid late fees and protect your credit score.

Paying your credit card bills on time is essential for maintaining a healthy financial life. With careful planning and budgeting, you can ensure that your bills are paid in full and on time each month.

Reducing Credit Card Balances:Reducing credit card balances is an important part of financial health. By reducing your credit card balance, you can improve your credit score, save on interest payments, and free up more money for other expenses.

The first step in reducing your credit card balance is to analyze your spending and determine where you can cut back. Look for ways to reduce your expenses, such as by shopping around for lower-cost services, reducing impulse purchases, and avoiding late fees.

Once you have identified areas for spending reductions, it's time to start paying down your credit card balance. Make a budget and set aside a certain amount each month for credit card payments. Consider making extra payments whenever you can, or setting up automatic payments so that the payment is made on time each month.

If you have multiple credit cards, you may want to focus on paying off the card with the highest interest rate first.

also consider consolidating your credit card debt. Consolidating your debt can help you reduce your interest rate, which can help you save on interest payments. It can also make it easier to track your payments and keep up with your monthly payments.

Finally, it is important to keep up with your credit card payments. Paying your balance in full each month is the best way to avoid interest charges and late fees. It also helps you maintain a good credit score, which can be useful when applying for loans or other financial products.

Reducing credit card balances is an important part of managing your finances. By following these tips, you can save money, improve your credit score, and free up more money for other expenses.

Keeping Credit Card Utilization Low:Keeping credit card utilization low is an important part of maintaining good credit.Generally, credit card companies and credit bureaus recommend keeping your utilization below 30%, with lower numbers being even better.

The main benefit of keeping your credit card utilization low is that it helps you maintain a good credit score. Credit card utilization is one of the factors used to determine credit score. Higher utilization rates can lead to lower credit scores and make it harder to get loans or other lines of credit.

There are several ways to keep your credit card utilization low. The most obvious is to pay off your balance in full every month. If you are unable to do this, you can make multiple payments throughout the month to keep your utilization low. You can also request a higher credit limit from your credit card company, which will increase the total amount of credit available and lower your utilization rate. Finally, you can spread your purchases out across multiple cards to help keep utilization low.

No matter what approach you take, it's important to remember that keeping credit card utilization low is a key part of maintaining a good credit score. By following the tips and strategies outlined above, you can keep your credit card utilization low and protect your credit score.

Avoiding Excessive Applications for Credit:Avoiding excessive applications for credit is an important part of maintaining healthy credit. Applying for too much credit in a short period of time can hurt your credit score and make it difficult to get approved for new credit. The more applications you have, the more inquiries appear on your credit report, which can lower your rating.

When you apply for credit, it's important to make sure you're not applying for too much. Consider the offers you get from lenders carefully, and make sure you meet the criteria for approval. If you don't, you may be rejected for the loan or credit card and this could have a negative impact on your credit score.

Finally, it's important to read the fine print when applying for credit. Make sure you understand the terms and conditions of the loan or credit card you're applying for. This can help you avoid excessive fees or other costly surprises down the line.

By avoiding excessive applications for credit, you can help protect your credit score and maintain a healthy financial profile. Be sure to read the fine print and space out your applications to ensure you're making the right decisions for your financial future.

Managing Credit Responsibly:Managing credit responsibly is a key part of financial health. When done right, credit can be a great tool for building wealth and security. However, if not managed properly, credit can become a source of financial stress and burden.

The first step to managing credit responsibly is to be aware of how credit works. Knowing the terms and conditions of any credit agreement is important. It is important to understand how interest rates, fees, and other charges affect the total cost of credit. It is also important to understand how payment history affects credit scores.

The second step is to use credit responsibly. This means staying within the credit limit, making regular payments on time, and avoiding overspending. It also means limiting the number of credit cards and loans used. Limiting the number of credit cards makes it easier to track spending and reduces the risk of missing payments.

The third step is to monitor credit regularly. Checking credit reports and scores gives insight into credit utilization, payment history, and other factors that affect credit scores. Regularly monitoring credit helps to identify and address potential issues.A budget is an important tool for managing finances and credit responsibly. It helps to identify areas

Reviewing Your Credit Reports:Reviewing your credit reports is an important step in managing your finances and protecting your financial health. Credit reports contain information on your credit history, including your payment history, debt levels, and any accounts that have been opened or closed in your name. This information is used by lenders and creditors to determine your creditworthiness and assess the risk of granting you a loan or line of credit.

By reviewing your credit reports, you can identify any inaccurate or incomplete information that could be damaging your credit score. This is especially important if you are applying for a loan or other financing, as lenders will use your credit reports to determine whether you are a good candidate for their services.

It is recommended that you review your credit reports at least once a year to ensure accuracy and to identify any potential signs of identity theft.

Disputing Errors on Credit Reports:Disputing errors on credit reports can be a daunting task. It is important to remember that credit reporting agencies are responsible for reporting accurate information, and it is possible to challenge any information that appears to be incorrect.Get a copy of your credit report. Once you have your credit report, you should review it carefully and identify any errors you believe to be present. Once you have identified the errors, you should contact the credit reporting agency to explain the discrepancy and request a correction.

When disputing errors on a credit report, be sure to include any supporting documentation that may be necessary to prove your case. This could include bank statements, credit card statements, or any other relevant documents that prove the information on your credit report is incorrect.

When disputing errors, it is also important to be patient. The credit reporting agencies must investigate any disputes, so it may take some time before you receive any results.

Once the dispute process is complete, the credit reporting agencies must correct any errors they find. If they do not, you may be able to take legal action against them.

Disputing errors on credit reports can be a long and frustrating process. However, it is an important step in protecting your credit score and ensuring your credit report is accurate.

Resolving Credit Disputes:When it comes to resolving credit disputes, the key is to stay organized and be persistent. The best way to do this is to keep all of your documents, including the dispute letter and any documents you may receive in response.

To start the process, you should contact the disputed creditor by mail, phone, or email. When you contact them, make sure to provide as much documentation as possible. This could include copies of your credit report, a copy of the dispute letter, and copies of any documents that show proof of the dispute.

Once you have contacted the creditor, they will typically respond with a letter or other form of communication. This letter will outline the dispute and provide more information on how the dispute will be resolved.

It is important to read the letter carefully and respond promptly. If the creditor is not willing to resolve the dispute in your favor, you may need to take the dispute to the next level and file a dispute with the credit bureaus.

When filing a dispute with the credit bureaus, it is important to provide as much information as possible. This includes a copy of the dispute letter, copies of any documents that show proof of the dispute, and any other information that could help the credit bureaus make decisions.

Once you have filed the dispute, the credit bureaus will review the documentation and make a decision. If they find in your favor, they will update your credit report and the disputed account will be removed.

If the credit bureaus do not find in your favor, you may need to take the dispute to the next level. This could include filing a complaint with the Consumer Financial Protection Bureau or even filing a lawsuit against the disputed creditor.

Regardless of the outcome, it is important to stay organized and be persistent when resolving credit disputes. By following this advice, you can ensure that the dispute is resolved in your favor.

Monitoring Your Credit Score:Monitoring your credit score is an important step in managing your financial health. Regularly checking your credit score allows you to identify any negative changes in your credit history and take corrective action quickly. It also helps you to understand what factors are impacting your credit score and work to improve them.

Monitoring your credit score is easy and can be done through a number of sources including credit bureaus and credit monitoring services. Checking your credit score periodically can help you detect any errors or fraudulent activity that could be damaging your score, as well as alert you to signs of identity theft. Additionally, monitoring your credit score can help you understand how loan and credit card applications are impacting your score, allowing you to make more informed decisions about the types of credit products you apply for.

You should also be aware of the importance of monitoring your credit score regularly. A credit score is a snapshot of your financial health and can have a major impact on your ability to qualify for loans, credit cards, and other types of financial products. Regularly monitoring your credit score can help you stay on top of changes in your score, giving you the opportunity to make adjustments to your financial habits and activities as needed.

Protecting Your Credit:Protecting your credit is an important aspect of managing your finances and maintaining a good credit score. There are a few steps you can take to protect your credit rating and ensure that your credit score remains high and your personal information remains secure.

First, it is important to be aware of what is going on with your credit score and to regularly monitor it. You can do this by viewing your credit report on a yearly basis. This will allow you to quickly detect any fraudulent activity or errors that may be present.

Second, it is important to keep your personal information secure. This means using strong passwords and avoiding giving out your credit card or account information to anyone who you do not trust. You should also be careful when clicking links in emails or responding to unsolicited phone calls or emails.

Third, you should be aware of any suspicious activity going on with your accounts. If you notice any sudden changes in your credit score or if you detect any unauthorized charges, it is important to contact the credit card company or bank immediately.

Finally, it is important to be careful when using your credit cards. Always be mindful of the amount of debt you are taking on and make sure to pay off your balances on time and in full. This will help to ensure that your credit score remains high and your financial situation stays secure.

By following these simple steps, you can protect your credit and ensure that your financial situation remains secure.

Safeguarding Your Personal Information:Safeguarding your personal information is an important step to take to protect yourself from identity theft. There are a few simple steps you can take to help protect your personal information and make sure it is not being used without your knowledge or consent.

The first step is to be aware of your personal information. Know what information you have, where it is stored, and who has access to it. You should also make sure that any personal information you have is stored securely and only shared with those who need it.

The next step is to be careful with your passwords. Make sure to use strong passwords that are long, unique, and difficult to guess.

Phishing scams occur when someone attempts to gain access to your personal information by pretending to be from a legitimate company or organization. Be sure to double-check any emails or websites you receive to ensure they are legitimate before providing any personal information.

Finally, it is important to use two-factor authentication whenever possible. This will require you to provide a second form of authentication, such as a code sent to your mobile phone, when logging into certain accounts. This provides an extra layer of security and can help protect your personal information.

It is important to be aware of your personal information and take steps to safeguard it.

Reporting Fraudulent Activity:

Reporting fraudulent activity is an important step to take in order to protect yourself and others. Fraudulent activity can range from identity theft to credit card fraud and many other types of financial crimes. It is important to report any suspicious activity as soon as possible in order to prevent further damage and to ensure that the proper authorities are notified.

If you suspect that you are a victim of fraud, the first step is to contact your local law enforcement agency. You can also contact your credit card company or bank to report the activity. Make sure to provide any information that you have, such as dates and account numbers.

You may also want to contact the Federal Trade Commission (FTC) or the Better Business Bureau to report the fraud. The FTC can investigate cases of identity theft, fraudulent online activities and other scams. The Better Business Bureau can provide advice and resources for victims of fraudulent activity.

It is important to keep records of all your communications with the authorities. This can be helpful in the event that you need to take further action, such as filing a police report or civil lawsuit.

Finally, it is important to take steps to protect yourself from future fraud. This includes monitoring your credit reports and accounts regularly, using strong passwords, and avoiding clicking on links in suspicious emails.

Freezing Your Credit:Freezing your credit is a way to protect your personal information from being used to open fraudulent accounts. When you freeze your credit, you prevent creditors from accessing your credit report and using it to make decisions about you. This is an especially important step for people who have been victims of identity theft or are concerned about their sensitive information falling into the wrong hands.

When you freeze your credit, you will receive a unique PIN from the credit bureaus that you must use when you want to access your credit report or take any other action that requires a credit check. You can also temporarily lift or thaw the freeze if you're applying for a loan or credit card, or if you need to access your credit report for any other reason.

Freezing your credit is a great way to protect your personal information and keep your finances secure. It's important to remember, though, that freezing your credit won't stop all forms of identity theft or fraud. You should still keep an eye on your credit report and bank statements and take other steps to protect your identity.

Avoiding Bad Credit Habits:Bad credit habits can have a long-lasting and damaging effect on your financial health. It is important to be aware of what practices can lead to bad credit and take steps to avoid them.

One bad credit habit to avoid is missing payments. Even if you are only a few days late, this can lead to late fees and a hit to your credit score. Make sure to pay bills on time and if necessary, set up payment reminders to help stay on top of them.

Another bad credit habit to avoid is carrying too much debt. Try to keep your debt-to-income ratio below 30%, as this will help you maintain a good credit score. If you are carrying too much debt, consider debt consolidation or other debt relief options to help bring your balance down.

Another bad credit habit to avoid is applying for too many credit cards or loans. Each time you apply for a new credit card or loan, it can cause a hard inquiry which will lower your credit score. Before applying for a new credit card or loan, make sure you understand the terms and conditions and shop around to get the best deal.

By avoiding these bad credit habits, you can help maintain a good credit score and be in a better position to take advantage of financial opportunities. Make sure to stay on top of your credit report and monitor your financial health to ensure you are making smart decisions.

Five

Investing basics

Investing is the process of putting money into assets such as stocks, bonds, mutual funds, real estate, and other investments with the expectation of earning a return. Investing provides the opportunity to create wealth over time by taking advantage of compounding returns. The goal of investing is to build a portfolio that can generate income or capital gains over time.

When investing, it is important to have a well-defined strategy that includes diversification, risk tolerance, investment time horizon, and financial goals. Diversification refers to spreading your money across different types of investments to reduce the risk of losing money. Risk tolerance is the amount of risk you are willing to take on in order to reach your financial goals. Investment time horizon is the length of time you plan to hold the investment before selling. Finally, financial goals refer to the specific goals you want to achieve with the money you invest.

It is also important to understand the different types of investments available and how they work. Stocks are shares of ownership of a company and offer the potential for capital gains and income in the form of dividends. Bonds are loans made to governments or corporations and offer the potential for fixed income. Mutual funds are collections of different types of investments and offer diversification. Real estate is an investment in physical property and generates returns in the form of rental income and capital gains.

Finally, it is important to understand the tax implications of investing. Different investments can be subject to different tax rates, so it is important to understand how taxes will affect your returns. In addition, it is important to understand the fees associated with investing, such as commissions, management fees, and other charges.

Investing can be a great way to generate wealth over time, but it is important to understand the basics before getting started. By having a well-defined strategy, understanding the types of investments available, and understanding the tax implications of investing, you can be sure that you are making well-informed decisions to help you reach your financial goals.

Basic investments

Investing can be one of the best ways to grow your money, but it can also be daunting if you're new to it. It's important to remember that investing is a long-term strategy, so it's important to understand the basics before taking any risks. Here's a beginner's guide to basic investments:

1.Stocks are shares of ownership in a publicly traded corporation. They represent a claim on the company's assets and profits. When you purchase a stock, you become a part-owner of the company and are entitled to a portion of the company's profits and assets. By buying and selling stocks, investors can make money either through capital gains or dividends.

2.Bonds: Bonds are debt instruments issued by governments or corporations. When you buy a bond, you're essentially lending money to the issuer, and they will pay you a fixed rate of interest over a certain period of time. When the bond matures, you'll get your money back, plus the interest you've earned.

3.Mutual Funds: Mutual funds are investments that pool money from many investors and invest in a variety of stocks, bonds, and other assets. The benefit of investing in a mutual fund is that it's professionally managed and diversified, which can help reduce risk.

4.Exchange-Traded Funds (Etas): Etas are similar to mutual funds in that they're professionally managed and diversified. The difference is that Etas are traded on the stock exchange, so they can be bought and sold like stocks.

5.Real Estate: Investing in real estate can be a great way to generate passive income. You can purchase rental properties and rent them out to tenants, or you can invest in real estate development projects.

6.Bank Accounts: Bank accounts such as savings and checking accounts provide a safe and low-risk way of investing your money. The returns are usually low, but the risk is also low.

7.Commodities: Commodities are raw materials such as oil, gold, or wheat that can be bought and sold on exchanges. They can be a risky investment but can also offer potential profits.

8.Cryptocurrency: Cryptocurrencies such as Bitcoin are digital currencies that can be used for transactions. They are highly volatile and can offer high returns but also come with high risk.

9.Options: Options are financial contracts that give the buyer the right to buy or sell an asset at a predetermined price. They can be a speculative investment and can involve high risk.

10.Precious Metals: Investing in precious metals such as gold, silver, and platinum can offer a hedge against inflation. They can also offer capital gains in the long term.

As you become more familiar with investing, you can explore other options such as futures, commodities, and options. It's important to do your research and invest wisely.

10 benefits of basic investments

1. Access to Long-term Goals: By investing a portion of their income, individuals can better ensure their access to long-term goals, such as retirement or college tuition.

2. Growth Potential: Investing allows individuals to take advantage of the growth potential of their investments. This can be done through a variety of vehicles, such as stocks, bonds, mutual funds, and more.

3. Diversification: Investing allows individuals to diversify their portfolio, reducing the risk associated with investing in any single asset.

4. Tax Benefits: Investing can provide tax benefits, as investments can be sheltered from taxes.

5. Compounding Interest: Investing can provide compounding interest, allowing investments to grow and earn more money over time.

6. Higher Returns: Investing can provide higher returns than would be earned from a savings account or other low-risk investments.

7. Financial Security: Investing can provide individuals with financial security, as investments can help to provide an additional source of income.

8. Financial Education: Investing can help individuals to become more financially savvy, as it provides the opportunity to learn about markets, investment vehicles, and more.

9. Professional Advice: Investing can provide access to professional advice, which can help investors make more informed decisions.

10. Flexibility: Investing can provide flexibility, as investments can be tailored to meet individual needs and goals.

Six

retirement planning

Retirement planning is an important part of a secure financial future. Planning for retirement is a complex process that requires careful consideration of many factors, including the amount of money you will need to live comfortably in retirement, how much you will need to save each month to reach that goal, and what types of investments you should make to ensure that your money will last throughout your retirement years.

When planning for retirement, it's important to consider your current income, expenses, and lifestyle. Knowing how much you will need to live comfortably in retirement will help you determine the amount of money you need to save each month. You should also consider other sources of income, such as Social Security, pensions, and other retirement savings accounts.

In addition to considering your current financial situation, you should also think about your future needs. This includes accounting for inflation, medical expenses, long-term care costs, and other unforeseen expenses in retirement. You should also consider how you will adjust your lifestyle and expenses in retirement, as your income may be lower than it was before.

When it comes to investing for retirement, it's important to develop an investment strategy that meets your individual needs. You should consider your risk tolerance, time horizon, and goals when choosing investments that will help you reach your retirement goals. It's also important to diversify your investments to reduce your risk and ensure that your money will last throughout your retirement years.

Finally, it's important to review your retirement plan regularly to make sure you're on track to reach your goals. A financial advisor can help you identify any potential issues or changes that need to be made to your retirement plan.

Retirement planning can seem overwhelming, but it's essential to ensuring a secure financial future. With careful planning and the right investments, you can enjoy a comfortable retirement.

There are five primary types of retirement planning strategies: saving, investing, Social Security, annuities, and pensions.

Saving: Saving for retirement involves setting aside money in a variety of different accounts specifically designed for retirement.

These accounts are typically tax-advantaged and may include 401(k)s, IRAs, Roth IRAs, and tax-free savings accounts.

Investing: Investing for retirement involves getting involved in different types of investments, such as stocks, bonds, mutual funds, and exchange-traded funds (Etas). The goal of investing is to grow the value of your retirement accounts with the help of asset appreciation and income from interest or dividends.

Social Security: Social Security is a government-backed retirement program that provides a monthly benefit to qualified individuals who are retired or disabled. Depending on your age and work history, you may be eligible for Social Security benefits.

Annuities: An annuity is an insurance product that provides a guaranteed stream of income for a certain period of time or for the rest of your life. Annuities can be fixed or variable, and they can be structured in a variety of ways.

Pensions: A pension is an employer-sponsored retirement plan that provides a guaranteed stream of income for life. Pensions are usually funded by the employer and are typically paid out on a monthly basis.

Retirement planning is an important part of financial planning. By implementing the right strategies, you can ensure that you have enough money to enjoy a comfortable retirement.

Seven

Insurance

Insurance is a way to protect yourself and your family from financial losses due to unforeseen circumstances, such as death, illness, property damage, or legal liability. Insurance provides an economic safety net to help cover the costs associated with these situations.

The most common type of insurance is health insurance, which helps cover the costs associated with medical care. Health insurance plans vary widely in terms of coverage levels, deductibles, and premiums. Employer-sponsored health insurance is the most common form of health insurance, although many individuals purchase private health insurance on their own.

Auto insurance is another common type of insurance. Auto insurance helps cover the costs associated with damage to your car, as well as liability for any injuries or property damage that you may cause.

Auto insurance is typically required in order to legally operate a vehicle.

Property insurance is also widely used to protect homes and other valuable items against damage caused by natural disasters, theft, and other events. Property insurance policies typically include coverage for the replacement cost of any damaged items.

Finally, life insurance is a type of insurance that provides financial protection for your family in the event of your death. Life insurance policies provide a death benefit to your beneficiaries, which can be used to help pay for funeral costs, medical bills, and other expenses.

Insurance is an important financial tool that can help protect you and your family from unforeseen events. By understanding the basics of insurance and the different types of coverage available, you can ensure that you have the right protection in place to help you and your family in case of an emergency.

Benefits of Insurance Basics

1. Financial Security: Insurance offers financial protection in the event of an unexpected loss or injury. It helps provide a financial safety net for individuals and families and helps them to recover from losses and rebuild their lives.

2. Peace of Mind: Insurance offers peace of mind for individuals and families by providing financial protection in the event of an

unexpected loss or injury. It also helps protect against the financial risks associated with accidents and illnesses.

3. Risk Management: Insurance helps to manage and reduce the financial risks of unexpected losses or injuries. It also helps to protect individuals and families from the financial impacts of catastrophic events, such as fires, floods, and other disasters.

4. Retirement Planning: Insurance can be used to help individuals and families plan for their retirement. Through the use of life insurance and annuities, individuals and families can save for their retirement and ensure that they have enough money to cover their expenses in the future.

5. Tax Benefits: Insurance offers tax benefits for individuals and families. Life insurance and annuities are both tax-advantaged investments, meaning that the money saved in them is not subject to income taxes, and the money earned from them is taxed at a lower rate. This can save individuals and families money and help them to reach their financial goals.

There are many types of insurance available, including health, life, auto, and property. Health insurance provides coverage for medical expenses incurred due to illness or injury, while life insurance provides coverage for death or disability. Auto insurance covers damage to vehicles and property resulting from an accident, as well as liability costs from an accident. Property insurance covers damage to property and personal possessions due to fire, theft, or natural disaster.

In addition to these more common types of insurance, there are many specialty types of insurance available. These policies may provide coverage for specific risks, such as pet insurance, travel insurance, or professional liability insurance. Specialty policies are often tailored to meet the needs of individuals or businesses.

No matter what type of insurance you need, it is important to understand the terms of the policy and to select a policy with the appropriate coverage. It is also important to review your policy regularly to ensure that it still meets your needs.

Tax Planning

Tax planning is the analysis of various tax options in order to minimize a tax liability. It is a legal and ethical process of arranging financial affairs in order to minimize taxes. The goal of tax planning is to reduce or eliminate taxes, while still complying with the law. Tax planning involves strategies that maximize deductions and credits while minimizing taxes.

Tax planning strategies typically involve taking advantage of deductions, credits, and other tax incentives that are available to taxpayers. Some tax planning strategies may involve deferring or accelerating income or expenses, or making certain investments in order to reduce tax liability. Taxpayers may also use tax planning strategies to optimize the timing of certain types of income or expenses in order to maximize their tax savings.

Tax planning should take into consideration both the short-term and long-term effects of the strategies being used. It is important to consider the tax implications of any decision in order to ensure that the strategies used are not only beneficial in the short-term, but also beneficial in the long-term.

Eight

Tax planning

Tax planning should be done on an ongoing basis in order to ensure that the strategies used are still beneficial. It is important to review and analyze tax laws and regulations regularly in order to stay up to date with the latest changes. Tax planning should also be done in coordination with other financial planning strategies in order to ensure that the overall financial goals are met.

Types of tax planning

Tax planning is the process of structuring one's financial affairs in order to minimize the amount of income tax owed. It can involve rearranging one's investments, business activities, and other financial decisions in order to reduce the amount of tax owed. There are various types of tax planning strategies available depending on an individual's financial situation and goals.

1. Income Shifting: Income shifting is a strategy used to reduce taxes by transferring income from one person to another in a lower tax bracket. This is often done through the use of trusts, family partnerships, and other entities.

2. Charitable Donations: Charitable donations can be used to reduce the amount of taxes owed by allowing individuals to deduct the value of the donation from their taxable income. This is especially beneficial for those in higher tax brackets.

3. Tax Deferral: Tax deferral is a strategy used to delay the payment of taxes until a later date in the future. This is often done through the use of retirement accounts and other investment vehicles.

4. Tax Credits: Tax credits are a form of tax relief that can be used to reduce the amount of taxes owed. Examples of tax credits include the earned income tax credit, the child tax credit, and the education tax credit.

5. Tax Loss Harvesting: Tax loss harvesting is a strategy used to offset capital gains with losses from other investments. This can help reduce the amount of taxes owed on capital gains.

6. Tax-Free Investment Accounts: Tax-free investment accounts such as Roth IRAs and Health Savings Accounts can be used to shelter income from taxes. These accounts are often used to save for retirement or medical expenses.

7. Offshore Tax Planning: Offshore tax planning is a strategy used to take advantage of lower tax rates in other countries. This is often done by individuals and businesses that have operations in multiple countries.

Tax planning can be a complex process, and it is important to consult a tax professional to ensure you are taking advantage of all available tax planning strategies.

Benefits of tax planning

Tax planning is a critical part of financial planning, as it allows individuals and businesses to take advantage of tax incentives, deductions and credits. Tax planning can help to lower your overall tax liability, which can lead to greater savings and more income. Here are some of the key benefits of tax planning:

1. Better Financial Planning: Tax planning can help you to identify deductions and credits that you may be eligible for, allowing you to save money in the long-term. By utilizing tax planning services, you can gain an understanding of your current financial situation and develop a better plan for the future.

2. Lower Taxes: Tax planning can help to reduce your overall tax liability by identifying tax deductions and credits that may apply to your situation. This can lead to a lower tax bill and more money in your pocket.

3. Avoid Tax Penalties: Tax planning can help you to avoid costly tax penalties by ensuring that you are making the right decisions. Tax planning can help you to stay on track with filing your taxes on time and avoiding any potential problems.

4. Planning For Retirement: Tax planning can help you to plan for retirement, as it can provide you with information on how to maximize your retirement savings. Tax planning can help you to understand the different types of accounts, such as 401(k)s and IRAs, and how to take advantage of them.

5. Legal Protection: Tax planning can help you to reduce the risk of being audited by the IRS, as it can help you to make sure that you are following the rules and regulations of the tax system. This can provide you with the legal protection that you need in the event of an audit.

Overall, tax planning can be a great tool for individuals and businesses to take advantage of in order to maximize their savings and reduce their overall tax liability. It is important to work with a qualified tax professional to ensure that you are taking full advantage of all the benefits that tax planning can provide.

Managing Your Finances for the Future

Managing your finances for the future is a crucial part of making sure you have a secure and comfortable life. It can be intimidating to think about planning for your future, but with the right steps, you can create a plan that will help you achieve your financial goals.

The first step in managing your finances for the future is to create a budget. A budget will help you track your income and expenses, so you can see where your money is going and where you need to make adjustments. To create a budget, you need to decide how much you want to save each month, calculate your monthly income and expenses, and adjust your budget as needed.

Once you have a budget, you should look into saving and investing. Saving money will help you build a financial cushion for unexpected expenses, while investing can help you grow your wealth over time. When it comes to investing, you should do your research and find an investment strategy that fits your risk tolerance and financial goals.

In addition to saving and investing, you should also make sure you stay on top of your debts. Paying off debt can help you reduce your financial burden and set yourself up for success in the future. Make sure to pay more than the minimum payment on any loans or credit card bills you may have, and if possible, try to pay them off as quickly as you can.

Finally, it's important to make sure you have an emergency fund. An emergency fund is a set amount of money you save in case of an emergency. Having an emergency fund will help you avoid taking on debt if an unexpected expense arises.

Managing your finances for the future can be intimidating, but with the right steps, you can create a plan that will help you achieve your financial goals. Start by creating a budget, saving and investing, paying off debts, and setting up an emergency fund. With these steps, you can make sure you are prepared for whatever the future may bring.

11 Ways to managing your finance

1.Save for Retirement: Saving for retirement is essential for anyone looking to secure their financial future. Setting aside money each month for retirement can help you to accumulate a nest egg that will serve you well in your later years.

2.Make Smart Purchases: Making smart purchases is an important part of financial management. Always make sure to research products before making any purchases so that you can make sure you are getting value for your money.

3.Avoid Debt: Avoiding debt is essential for managing your finances. Debt can be a heavy burden and can prevent you from achieving your financial goals.

4.Use Credit Cards Wisely: Credit cards can be a great tool for managing your finances if used wisely. Always make sure to pay off your credit card balance each month in order to avoid accumulating high interest rates.

5.Protect Your Identity: Protecting your identity is essential for financial management. Make sure you protect your social security number and other personal information to avoid identity theft.

6.Create an Emergency Fund: An emergency fund is essential for managing your finances. Having an emergency fund will help you to cover unexpected expenses and prevent you from relying on credit cards.

7.Monitor Your Credit Score: Monitoring your credit score is essential for managing your finances. Having a good credit score will help you to get the best rates when borrowing money or applying for a loan.

8.Stick to Your Goals: Sticking to your financial goals is essential for financial management. Having a plan and sticking to it will help you to reach your long-term objectives.

9.Automate Your Finances: Automating your finances is a great way to make sure your bills are paid on time and that you are staying within your budget.

10.Cut Unnecessary Expenses: Cutting unnecessary expenses is an important part of financial management. Identifying and eliminating any unnecessary expenses can help you to save money and reach your financial goals.

11.Seek Professional Advice: Seeking professional advice is an important part of financial management. A financial advisor can help you to identify areas of your finances that need improvement and create a plan for achieving your financial goals.

Building wealth

Wealth is defined as having a large amount of money, property, and other material possessions. Building wealth can be a great way to secure your financial future, as having a source of income that can sustain you is essential for long-term security. There are multiple benefits to building wealth, such as providing financial freedom, growing your retirement savings, and having more time to spend doing the things you love.

Strategies to Build Wealth

The key to building wealth is to ensure you are taking the right steps to build your financial future. Investing is one of the most common and effective ways to build wealth, and it helps to diversify your portfolio and minimize risk. Budgeting is also an important factor in building wealth, as tracking your expenses and setting financial goals can help you reach your desired level of financial security. Finally, saving money regularly is an excellent way to build wealth, as having a rainy day fund and other savings accounts can help you prepare for unexpected expenses.

Challenges to Building Wealth

Building wealth can be difficult, and there are many challenges that can arise. A lack of knowledge or experience in the financial markets can make it difficult to be successful. Additionally, market volatility can cause unexpected losses and make it difficult to reach your financial goals. Finally, unforeseen expenses can disrupt your budget and make it difficult to save for the future.

Benefits of Building Wealth:

Building wealth can be a great way to provide financial stability and security for yourself and your family. Here are some of the benefits of building wealth:

1. Financial Freedom: Building wealth allows you to become financially independent and free from the rat race of working for someone ease's money. You can build enough wealth to support yourself and your family without having to worry about being in debt or worrying about money.

2. Security: Building wealth can provide a sense of security and peace of mind that you and your family's future is secure. Having a nest egg of savings or investments can help protect you from economic downturns and provide a cushion in case of a financial emergency.

3. Retirement Savings: Building wealth can give you the freedom to retire when you'd like and still have enough income to support yourself. Having a nest egg of investments and savings can provide you with a reliable source of income in retirement, so you don't have to worry about running out of money.

4. Generational Wealth: Building wealth can help you pass on financial security to future generations. You can start investing in your children's education and help them build wealth of their own.

5. Tax Benefits: Investing in certain types of investments can provide you with tax benefits, such as capital gains tax exemptions or deductions.

Building wealth can be a great way to secure your financial future and ensure you and your family are taken care of. You can use the money to invest in yourself and your future, or you can use it to help others in need.

Strategies to Build Wealth :strategies to building wealth

1. Start Early: The earlier you start building wealth, the more time you have to benefit from the power of compounding. Compounding is the process of earning interest on your investments and then reinvesting that interest to earn even more interest. Starting early gives you more time to benefit from compounding, which is the key to building wealth over time.

2. Live Below Your Means: Living below your means is a key component of building wealth. This means spending less than you earn and saving the difference.

3. Invest Wisely: Investing your money wisely is essential to building wealth. It's important to diversify your investments and have a mix of stocks, bonds, and other investments to ensure you're taking advantage of the different markets and asset classes.

4. Have a Plan: Creating a plan for how you want to build wealth is important. This plan should include your short-term and long-term financial goals and how you plan to reach those goals. Having a plan in place will help keep you on track and make sure you're working towards your goals.

5. Automate Your Savings: Automating your savings is a great way to ensure that you're putting money away regularly. You can set up automatic transfers from your checking account to your savings or investment accounts each month so you don't have to worry about manually transferring the money each month.

6. Take Calculated Risks: Taking calculated risks is essential when it comes to investing. Investing in stocks and other investments carries some risk, but if you do your research and understand the market, you can make informed decisions about which investments to make.

7. Stay The Course: Building wealth takes time and patience. It's important to stay the course and not get too caught up in day-to-day

fluctuations in the markets. The key is to stay focused on your long-term goals and continue to invest and save consistently.

Challenges to Building Wealth:Building wealth is a difficult challenge for many Americans. It requires a great deal of discipline and hard work. Here are some of the most common challenges to building wealth:

1. Debt: Debt can be a major hindrance to building wealth. High-interest rates, late fees, and compounding debt can quickly eat away at any progress made towards building wealth.

2. Lack of Investment Knowledge: Many people lack the knowledge and experience needed to make sound investments. This can lead to poor decisions that can quickly sabotage any attempt to build wealth.

3. Inadequate Savings: It is important to save as much as possible, but many people are unable to do so. Not having enough money set aside for emergency expenses or for retirement can be a major obstacle in building wealth.

4. Market Volatility: The stock market can be unpredictable, and major losses can occur quickly. This can make it difficult to build wealth through investments.

5. Lack of Diversification: Building wealth requires diversifying investments across different asset classes. Without diversification, a portfolio can be exposed to significant risk.

6. Poor Financial Habits: Poor financial habits can quickly erode any efforts to build wealth. Things like spending more than you make, impulse buying, and neglecting to save can be major impediments to wealth building.

These are just some of the challenges to building wealth. With the right strategies and discipline, however, it is possible to overcome these obstacles and build a secure financial future.

Lack of Knowledge:Lack of knowledge can have a significant impact on an individual's life. It can limit their opportunities, affect their decision-making, and lead to a lack of understanding of the world around them. Without knowledge, individuals are unable to make informed decisions, which can lead to costly mistakes. Additionally, without knowledge, individuals are unable to take advantage of the resources available to them.

In addition to the impact on the individual, lack of knowledge can have a negative impact on society as a whole. When people are uninformed, they are more likely to make decisions that can harm the environment, create economic inequality, and lead to social injustice. When individuals are not properly educated on a subject, they are more likely to make decisions based on ignorance and fear, rather than facts and understanding.

Finally, lack of knowledge can also be harmful to personal relationships. When individuals do not have adequate knowledge of a subject, they may be unable to have meaningful conversations and connections with others. Without knowledge, individuals are unable to engage in meaningful dialogue with those around them, which can lead to misunderstandings and conflict.

Market Volatility:Market volatility is a measure of how much the price of a security or market index changes over a certain period of time. It is often used to measure risk and is a key factor in investing decisions. When markets are volatile, prices can move quickly and unpredictably, which can lead to large losses for investors who are not prepared for them. Volatility can also be caused by a variety of factors, such as economic news, political events, and other external influences.

Investors and traders often use volatility to their advantage. High levels of volatility can create opportunities for traders to take advantage of price swings and make profits. On the other hand, low levels of volatility can be a sign of a stagnant market with limited trading opportunities.

Volatility can also be an indicator of market sentiment. When markets are volatile, investors tend to be more cautious and less willing to take risks. This can lead to a decrease in trading volumes and a decrease in overall market liquidity.

In summary, market volatility is an important factor for investors and traders to consider when making decisions about their investments. It can provide key insights about market sentiment and can be used to take advantage of opportunities created by price movements.

Unforeseen Expenses:Unforeseen expenses can be stressful and difficult to manage. They can arise from a variety of sources, such as unexpected medical bills, vehicle repairs, or home maintenance costs. It's important to be prepared for these unexpected expenses by having an emergency fund and budgeting for them in advance.

Creating an emergency fund is a great way to prepare for unforeseen expenses. This fund should be used to pay for any unexpected costs that arise and should include at least three to six months' worth of living expenses. This fund should be kept in a separate account and not be used for everyday expenses.

In addition to having an emergency fund, budgeting for unforeseen expenses is also important. This can be done by setting aside a certain amount of money each month to cover unexpected costs. This amount should be included in your overall budget so that you're not caught off guard if an unexpected bill arrives.

Finally, it's important to stay informed on your finances. You should regularly review your accounts and credit reports to make sure that bills are being paid on time and that you're staying on top of any unexpected costs. This way, you'll be better prepared to handle any surprises that may come up.

Conclusion

Building wealth is essential for long-term financial security, and it can provide you with many benefits. While there are many strategies to build wealth, such as investing, budgeting, and saving, there are also many challenges that can arise. With dedication and the right knowledge, however, building wealth can be a rewarding and   successful   endeavor.

Nine

Managing your finance for the future

Managing Your Finances for the Future

Managing your finances for the future is a crucial part of making sure you have a secure and comfortable life. It can be intimidating to think about planning for your future, but with the right steps, you can create a plan that will help you achieve your financial goals.

The first step in managing your finances for the future is to create a budget. A budget will help you track your income and expenses, so you can see where your money is going and where you need to make adjustments. To create a budget, you need to decide how much you want to save each month, calculate your monthly income and expenses, and adjust your budget as needed.

Once you have a budget, you should look into saving and investing. Saving money will help you build a financial cushion for unexpected expenses, while investing can help you grow your wealth over time. When it comes to investing, you should do your research and find an investment strategy that fits your risk tolerance and financial goals.

In addition to saving and investing, you should also make sure you stay on top of your debts. Paying off debt can help you reduce your financial burden and set yourself up for success in the future. Make sure to pay more than the minimum payment on any loans or credit card bills you may have, and if possible, try to pay them off as quickly as you can.

Finally, it's important to make sure you have an emergency fund. An emergency fund is a set amount of money you save in case of an emergency. Having an emergency fund will help you avoid taking on debt if an unexpected expense arises.

Managing your finances for the future can be intimidating, but with the right steps, you can create a plan that will help you achieve your financial goals. Start by creating a budget, saving and investing, paying off debts, and setting up an emergency fund. With these steps, you can make sure you are prepared for whatever the future may bring.

11 Ways to managing your finance

1.Save for Retirement: Saving for retirement is essential for anyone looking to secure their financial future. Setting aside money each month for retirement can help you to accumulate a nest egg that will serve you well in your later years.

2.Make Smart Purchases: Making smart purchases is an important part of financial management. Always make sure to research products before making any purchases so that you can make sure you are getting value for your money.

3.Avoid Debt: Avoiding debt is essential for managing your finances. Debt can be a heavy burden and can prevent you from achieving your financial goals.

4.Use Credit Cards Wisely: Credit cards can be a great tool for managing your finances if used wisely. Always make sure to pay off your credit card balance each month in order to avoid accumulating high interest rates.

5.Protect Your Identity: Protecting your identity is essential for financial management. Make sure you protect your social security number and other personal information to avoid identity theft.

6.Create an Emergency Fund: An emergency fund is essential for managing your finances. Having an emergency fund will help you to cover unexpected expenses and prevent you from relying on credit cards.

7.Monitor Your Credit Score: Monitoring your credit score is essential for managing your finances. Having a good credit score will help you to get the best rates when borrowing money or applying for a loan.

8.Stick to Your Goals: Sticking to your financial goals is essential for financial management. Having a plan and sticking to it will help you to reach your long-term objectives.

9.Automate Your Finances: Automating your finances is a great way to make sure your bills are paid on time and that you are staying within your budget.

10.Cut Unnecessary Expenses: Cutting unnecessary expenses is an important part of financial management. Identifying and eliminating any unnecessary expenses can help you to save money and reach your financial goals.

11.Seek Professional Advice: Seeking professional advice is an important part of financial management. A financial advisor can help you to identify areas of your finances that need improvement and create a plan for achieving your financial goals.

Ten

Building wealth

Building wealth is a long term process that requires dedication and discipline. It is important to establish a budget and stick to it in order to save money. Investing money in the stock market, real estate, or other assets can help grow your wealth over time. It is also important to develop a diversified portfolio that can withstand market volatility.

Creating multiple streams of income can also help you build wealth. Having multiple sources of income will help you stay ahead of inflation and help you maintain financial security. This can include starting a side business, investing in dividend stocks, or renting out a property.

Finally, building wealth requires patience and consistency. You will need to make smart decisions and stay disciplined in order to see results. It may take years to reach your financial goals, but with dedication and hard work, you can create a strong financial foundation for years to come.

10 steps on how to build wealth

1. Create a Financial Plan: Taking a few hours to create a financial plan is one of the most important steps you can take on your journey to building wealth. Your plan should include a budget, long-term goals, an emergency fund, and an investment strategy.

2. Save Money: Start building wealth by setting aside a percentage of your income each month. Automate your savings to make sure it happens without fail. Make sure your savings are in an account that earns interest, such as a high-yield savings account.

3. Invest Wisely: Once you have an emergency fund in place, you can start investing your money. Investing in stocks, bonds, mutual funds, and index funds are all great options.

4. Pay Down Debt: If you have high-interest debt, such as credit card debt, paying it down should be a priority. Pay more than the minimum required payment to reduce your debt faster.

5. Build Passive Income: If you want to grow your wealth, you need to build passive income. Consider real estate investing, dividend investing, or launching an online business.

6. Live Below Your Means: If you want to build wealth, you need to live below your means. Stop making impulse purchases and focus on saving more money each month.

7. Protect Your Wealth: Make sure you have adequate insurance coverage to protect your wealth. Make sure you have life insurance, health insurance, and disability insurance.

8. Be Tax-Efficient: Make sure you are taking advantage of tax-advantaged accounts, such as a 401(k) or IRA. Consider hiring a financial advisor or accountant to help you with your tax planning.

9. Remain Patient: Building wealth takes time and patience. Don't expect to be wealthy overnight.

10. Give Back: Finally, don't forget to give back to your community. Consider donating to a charity or volunteering.

Eleven

Dealing with financial stress

Financial stress can be a very overwhelming and intimidating thing to deal with. The best way to tackle it is to take it one step at a time. Start by assessing your current financial situation. Make a list of your income and expenses and figure out how much money you have left over each month. Once you have a better understanding of how much money you have to work with, you can start looking for ways to reduce your expenses or increase your income.

Cutting back on unnecessary expenses, such as dining out or entertainment, can help you save money each month. On the other hand, if you are able to increase your income, such as taking on a second job or selling items online, you can use the extra money to pay off debt or build an emergency fund.

Once you have a better handle on your finances, you can focus on creating a budget. A budget will help you stay on track and ensure that you are meeting your financial goals. Setting up automatic payments for your bills can help ensure that you don't miss any due dates, which can help prevent late fees and penalties.

Finally, it is important to stay positive and have faith that things will get better. Talk to a financial planner or a trusted friend if you need support. Remember that financial stress is temporary, and with the right steps, you can get back on track.

10 ways on how to deal with financial stress

1. Identify the sources of financial stress: Identifying the sources of your financial stress is the first step in overcoming it. Common sources of financial stress include job insecurity, unexpected expenses, limited income, debt, and the fear of not having enough money.

2. Create a budget: Creating a budget is a great way to keep track of your income and expenses. This can help you identify spending habits that may be contributing to your financial stress and gives you a clearer picture of how much money you have available each month.

3. Cut back on spending: Cutting back on unnecessary expenses can help you reduce your financial stress. Identify areas in which you can limit spending, such as eating out and entertainment, and focus on only spending money on essential items.

4. Prioritize payments: Prioritizing your payments can help you manage your debts and reduce your financial stress. Make a list of all of your bills and prioritize them based on the amount due, interest rate, and due dates.

5. Set financial goals: Setting financial goals can help you stay focused on achieving your financial goals and provide you with a sense of accomplishment. Goals can be as simple as saving a certain amount of money each month or as complex as paying off your debt in a certain amount of time.

6. Talk to a financial planner: Seeking help from a financial planner can be a great way to reduce your financial stress. A financial planner can help you create a plan to achieve your financial goals and provide you with guidance to reach them.

7. Use free resources: There are many free resources available to help you manage your finances and reduce your financial stress. Many organizations offer free financial education, budgeting tools, and debt management services.

8. Take advantage of any available assistance: If you are experiencing financial hardship, there are a variety of government assistance programs that can help. These programs can provide assistance with housing, food, medical care, and more.

9. Consider changing jobs: If your job is a source of financial stress, consider changing jobs. Research different companies, review job

postings, and make sure the new job is a good fit for your skills and interests.

10. Seek support: Financial stress can be overwhelming, so don't be afraid to reach out for help. Talk to a friend or family member, join a support group, or seek professional help if needed.

Twelve

Protecting yourself from fraud

Protecting yourself from fraud requires vigilance and a proactive approach.

First, be aware of the common types of fraud, such as phishing, identity theft, and other scams. If you receive an email or a text message asking you to enter personal information or click on a link, be wary of the source.

Second, protect your data by creating strong passwords and changing them regularly. Avoid using the same password for multiple accounts and websites.

Third, be aware of the companies or websites you are dealing with. Research the company and its reputation before entering any financial information. Be wary of any website that does not use secure encryption technology.

Finally, if you suspect you have been a victim of fraud, contact your financial institution and the police immediately. Keep all records of the transaction and the details of the fraud, such as emails, website information, and any other evidence. Report the fraud to the Federal Trade Commission and the relevant authorities.

By taking these steps and remaining vigilant, you can help protect yourself from fraud.

20 ways of protecting yourself from fraud

1. Check your credit report regularly.

2. Monitor bank and credit card statements. Look for any suspicious activity and contact your bank or credit card provider immediately if you notice anything strange.

3. Avoid responding to emails that ask for your personal information.

4. Don't give out your Social Security Number, banking information, or passwords to anyone.

5. Never click on a link in an email or text message that you don't recognize.

6. Check offers that seem too good to be true.

7. Avior clicking on suspicious emails or text messages.

8. Don't give out personal information over the phone unless you initiated the call and you know who you're talking to.

9. Use strong passwords that are hard to guess.

10. Use a secure connection when shopping or banking online.

11. Use a credit card instead of a debit card when making purchases online.

12. Don't use public networks to access sensitive information.

13. Install and regularly update anti-virus and anti-malware software on your devices.

14. Use two-factor authentication if it's available.

15. Use a virtual private network (VAN) when accessing public WIFI.

16. Don't store your payment information on websites or apps.

17. Don't use the same password for multiple accounts.

18. Shred documents with personal information before disposing of them.

19. Be aware of phishing scams. Don't respond to emails or text messages from unknown senders.

20. Invest in an identity theft protection service

Thirteen

Working with financial professionals

F inancial professionals are essential for helping individuals and businesses make sound decisions about their money. Working with a financial professional can be beneficial, but it is important to take the time to understand the services they offer and to ensure that you have the right person for your needs.

What Is a Financial Professional?

A financial professional is a person who has experience and expertise in finance and investments. They can provide advice on a range of topics, such as budgeting, estate planning, retirement planning, and investments. Financial professionals come in many forms, such as Certified Financial Planners (C Fps), Chartered

Financial Analysts (Cf As), Registered Investment Advisors (IRAs), and more.

What Services Do Financial Professionals Offer?

Financial professionals offer a variety of services to their clients. Depending on the type of financial professional you work with, they may help you create an investing plan, review your insurance coverage, analyze your current investments, or recommend new investments. They can also provide advice on topics such as budgeting, taxes, retirement planning, and estate planning.

How to Choose a Financial Professional

When choosing a financial professional, it is important to do your research. Look for a professional who is qualified and accredited in your area, and who has experience in the topics you need help with. Ask for referrals from friends, family, and colleagues, and read reviews online. Make sure to understand all fees associated with their services.

Meeting with a Financial Professional

When you meet with a financial professional, it is important to be prepared. Have your financial documents ready, such as bank statements, tax returns, and investment information. Make sure you understand what services they provide, and what fees they charge.

Ask questions and make sure you understand the advice they are giving.

Working with a financial professional can help you make better decisions regarding your money and investments. By taking the time to find the right professional and understand their services, you can ensure that you are getting the best advice.

1. Use a Certified Financial Planner : is a professional who is certified to provide comprehensive financial planning advice. They can help you assess your current financial situation, create a plan to reach your goals, and provide ongoing guidance throughout your life.

2. Hire an Accountant: An accountant can help you manage your finances, prepare and file taxes, and make sure you are in compliance with applicable laws and regulations.

3. Invest in a Financial Advisor: Financial advisors can provide advice on investments, retirement planning, and tax planning. They can also provide guidance on asset allocation, risk management, and estate planning.

4. Work with a Certified Public Accountant (CPA): CPA's are qualified to offer financial advice and services, such as tax preparation, auditing, and financial statement preparation.

5. Utilize a Financial Consultant: Financial consultants can provide advice on investments, retirement planning, and portfolio management. They can also offer advice on asset protection, risk management, and estate planning.

6. Find a Financial Coach: Financial coaches can help you create a budget, set financial goals, and develop strategies to achieve them.

7. Use a Financial Planner: Financial planners can help you create an overall financial plan, set goals, and develop strategies to reach them.

8. Utilize a Financial Analyst: Financial analysts can provide research and analysis on investments, financial markets, and the economy.

9. Work with a Financial Strategist: Financial strategists can provide advice on investments, retirement planning, and estate planning.

10. Invest in a Tax Professional: Tax professionals can help you manage your taxes and ensure you are getting the best outcome when filing.

11. Utilize a Trust Officer: Trust officers can help you manage assets, investments, and trusts.

12. Get Financial Advice from an Investment Banker: Investment bankers can provide advice on investments, retirement planning, and portfolio management.

13. Use a Stockbroker: Stockbrokers can help you buy and sell stocks and other investments.

14. Seek Advice from an Insurance Agent: An insurance agent can provide advice on life insurance, health insurance, and other types of insurance.

15. Consult a Financial Litigator: Financial litigators can provide legal advice and representation on financial matters.

Fourteen

Making Smart Financial Decisions

Making smart financial decisions is key to achieving financial success. Smart financial decisions involve taking the time to understand your financial situation, setting realistic goals and developing a plan to reach them. It's important to stay disciplined and continue to make sound decisions so that you can achieve your financial goals.

The first step to making smart financial decisions is to calculate your net worth. This will give you an idea of the financial position you are in, and will help you understand the areas where you need to focus in order to improve your financial situation. Once you understand your net worth, you can begin setting goals to improve it. These goals should be realistic and achievable, and should be tailored to your own financial situation.

Once you have set your financial goals, it is important to develop a plan to reach them. This plan should include budgeting, setting aside money for savings and investing, and reducing debt. Budgeting will help you stay on track with your financial goals, while setting aside money for savings and investing will help you build wealth and reach your financial goals. Additionally, reducing debt will help you achieve financial success by freeing up money to invest and save.

Finally, it is important to stay disciplined and continue to make smart financial decisions. This means avoiding impulse purchases, creating an emergency fund, and staying up to date with changes to the economy and your own personal financial situation. Additionally, it is important to review and adjust your financial plan regularly to ensure that it still meets your goals.

Making smart financial decisions can help you achieve financial success and reach your goals. It is important to understand your financial situation, set realistic goals, and develop a plan to reach them. Additionally, it is important to stay disciplined and continue to make sound financial decisions. With the right plan and discipline, you can achieve your financial goals and enjoy financial success.

15 ways on how make smart financial decisions

1. Set Financial Goals: Before making any financial decisions, it is important to set realistic financial goals. Establishing goals helps to keep you on track and will provide a road map of where you want to go.

2. Create a Budget: A budget is essential for making smart financial decisions. It allows you to keep track of your income and expenses, and determine what you can afford to spend.

3. Live Within Your Means: One of the most important things to remember when making financial decisions is to live within your means. This means not spending more than you earn and avoiding unnecessary debt.

4. Make a Savings Plan: Establishing a savings plan is important for both short and long-term goals. Set aside a portion of your income each month to help you reach your financial goals.

5. Invest Wisely: Investing is an important part of making smart financial decisions. Research different investment options and make sure you understand the risks and rewards associated with each one.

6. Avoid Impulse Purchases: Impulse purchases can quickly drain your budget and derail your financial goals. Before making any purchases, take the time to think it through and determine if it's a necessary expense.

7. Pay Off Debt: Paying off debt should always be a priority when making financial decisions.

8. Monitor Your Credit: Regularly monitoring your credit report is essential for keeping your finances in order. Make sure to check for errors and report any discrepancies to the credit reporting agencies.

9. Plan for Retirement: Planning for retirement is an important part of making smart financial decisions. Start saving early and take advantage of employer retirement plans.

10. Take Advantage of Tax Benefits: Taking advantage of tax benefits can help maximize your financial returns. Investigate what tax deductions and credits you qualify for.

11. Shop Around for Insurance: Shopping around for insurance can help you find the best deal. Take the time to compare different policies and make sure you are getting the most coverage for the best price.

12. Negotiate: Don't be afraid to negotiate when making financial decisions. Whether you are purchasing a car or refinancing your mortgage, negotiating can help you get the best deal.

13. Research Before Making Major Purchases: Before making any major purchases, take the time to research the different options. This will help you make an informed decision and avoid any unnecessary costs.

14. Know Your Rights: Knowing your rights is important for making smart financial decisions. Take the time to educate yourself on consumer laws and regulations.

15. Seek Professional Advice: If you are unsure of how to handle your finances, it is always a good idea to seek professional advice. Look for a financial advisor who is knowledgeable and trustworthy.

www.ingramcontent.com/pod-product-compliance
Lightning Source LLC
Chambersburg PA
CBHW071137220526
45467CB00015B/1367